KT-196-052

C152019827

The *Shakespeare Library*

Shakespeare: A Life

WENDY GREENHILL

HEAD OF EDUCATION

ROYAL SHAKESPEARE COMPANY

and

PAUL WIGNALL

KENT
ARTS & LIBRARIES

C I 5 2 0 1 9 8 2 7

First published in Great Britain by Heinemann Library
Halley Court, Jordan Hill, Oxford OX2 8EJ
a division of Reed Educational & Professional Publishing Ltd

OXFORD FLORENCE PRAGUE MADRID ATHENS
MELBOURNE AUCKLAND KUALA LUMPUR SINGAPORE TOKYO
IBADAN NAIROBI KAMPALA JOHANNESBURG GABORONE
PORTSMOUTH NH (USA) CHICAGO MEXICO CITY SAO PAULO

© Reed Educational & Professional Publishing 1996

All rights reserved. No part of this publication may be reproduced, stored in a retrieval system, or transmitted
in any form by any means, electronic, mechanical, photocopying, recording, or otherwise without either the
prior written permission of the Publishers or a licence permitting restricted copying in the United Kingdom
issued by the Copyright Licensing Agency Ltd, 90 Tottenham Court Road, London W1P 9HE

Designed by Ken Vail Graphic Design, Cambridge
Printed in the UK by Jarrold Printing, Norwich

00 99 98 97 96
10 9 8 7 6 5 4 3 2 1

ISBN 0 431 07527 1

British Library Cataloguing in Publication Data
Greenhill, Wendy
Shakespeare: a life. – (The Shakespeare library)
1. Shakespeare, William, 1564–1616 – Biography – Juvenile literature 2. Dramatists, English – Early modern,
1500–1700 – Biography – Juvenile literature
I. Title II. Wignall, Paul
822.3'3

Acknowledgements
The authors and publishers would like to thank the following for permission to use
photographs and other illustrative material:

Berkeley Castle, Gloucestershire, page 20;
The Bridgeman Art Library, pages 19, 23;
The Bodleian Library, page 14;
The British Library, pages 16, 21;
Fotomas Index, page 9;
The National Portrait Gallery, pages 17, 25;
The Public Records Office, page 28;
The Royal Shakespeare Company, page 27;
The Shakespeare Centre Library: Stratford-upon-Avon, pages 4, 5, 6, 7, 8, 12, 13, 15, 26, 29, 31;
The Victoria and Albert Museum, page 11.

Cover photograph reproduced with permission of The National Portrait Gallery.

Our thanks to Jean Black and Andrew Gurr for their comments in the preparation of this book.

Every effort has been made to contact copyright holders of any material reproduced in this book. Any
omissions will be rectified in subsequent printings if notice is given to the Publisher.

CONTENTS

STRATFORD, 1564

SHAKESPEARE'S BIRTHPLACE

Stratford-upon-Avon is one of the most famous tourist attractions in the world. Every year hundreds of thousands of people come to see the house where William Shakespeare was born, the garden of the house where he died, and the church where he is buried. Many of those visitors will also see one of his plays performed in one of the Royal Shakespeare Company's three theatres.

Stratford is full of shops, car parks and cafés. Yet for all this modern bustle, we can still see something of William Shakespeare's town as it was during his lifetime. The pattern of streets remains much the same. There are still buildings in the town which he would have known. Even the busy atmosphere is not really new. In 1564, Stratford-upon-Avon was a thriving market town and an important river crossing for many travellers going between the Midlands and London.

Stratford-upon-Avon in 1759, based on a map drawn by Samuel Winter.

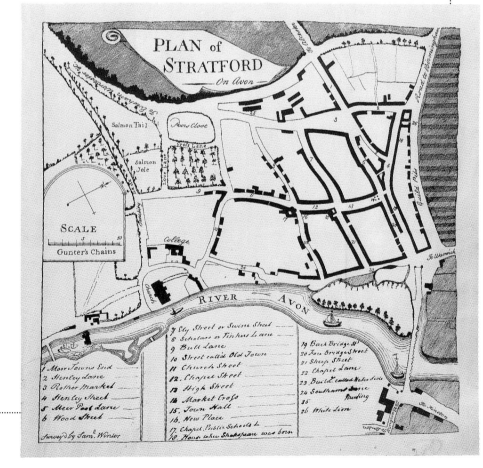

PLAN of STRATFORD
On Avon

SCALE
Gunter's Chains

RIVER AVON

1. Moor Towns End
2. Henley Lane
3. Rother Market
4. Henley Street
5. Meer Pool Lane
6. Wood Street
Survey'd by Sam. Winter

7. Ely Street or Swine Street
8. Scholars or Tinkers Lane
9. Bull Lane
10. Street call'd Old Town
11. Church Street
12. Chapel Street
13. High Street
14. Market Cross
15. Town Hall
16. New Place
17. Chapel, Public Schools &c.
18. House where Shakespeare was born

19. Back Bridge St.
20. Iron Bridge Street
21. Sheep Street
22. Chapel Lane
23. Build called Water Side
24. Southam Lane Bushing
25.
26. White Lion

SHAKESPEARE'S FAMILY

William's father, John Shakespeare, had come to Stratford in 1551 or 1552, and lived in a house in Henley Street. His own family were from Snitterfield, a village just north of Stratford. We know from the records of court hearings at that time that on 29 April 1552 he was fined (with others) for having a rubbish heap near his house instead of carting it to the town dump. John Shakespeare was a glover and 'whittawer' – that is, someone working with white leather. It was a skilled trade for which he would have worked as an apprentice, possibly for a Stratford glover, Thomas Dickson, before striking out on his own. He was obviously successful because in 1556 he bought the house next door to his in Henley Street and linked them to make one big house, now known as 'the Birthplace'. Stratford was by then an up-and-coming town. John Shakespeare was not going to be left behind.

John Shakespeare married in 1557 or early 1558. His wife was Mary Arden, the youngest of eight daughters of Robert Arden of Wilmcote, another village north of Stratford. The Ardens were prosperous farmers and Mary must have been a capable girl. When her father died in December 1556, she was responsible for dealing with his will. Two years later, aged 18, she married John Shakespeare and moved to Stratford, where she had many more responsibilities.

The wife of a sixteenth-century tradesman not only had to care for her husband and children, but was also expected to run the business when he wasn't there. Mary would have had to know about tanning and preparing leather as well as glove-making, and would also have needed the confidence to stand up to her husband's apprentices and employees, and other tradesmen in the town.

John and Mary Shakespeare's first two children, Joan and Margaret, died as babies. Such early death was not unusual in those days when there was no protection against childhood illness. In fact it is remarkable that their next child, William, survived at all. He was born when the plague was raging in Stratford. That year nearly 15 per cent of the town's population died – struck down by the killer disease – including four children of Richard Green, a miller who lived two doors away from the Shakespeares.

It is possible that William Shakespeare was born on 23 April 1564. That is the date celebrated around the world, and in Stratford there are processions and special events. But all we know for sure is that Stratford parish baptism records read:

> **1564 April 26 Gulielmus filius Johannes Shakspere**
>
> **(1564 April 26 William son of John Shakspere)**

JOHN SHAKESPEARE
'A MERRY CHEEKED OLD MAN'

The Elizabethans were an argumentative lot who made much use of the law to settle their disputes. The records of these court hearings, as well as other legal documents such as wills and the papers to do with purchase of houses or land, give us most of our information about ordinary life in those days.

John was also involved in farming his father's land in Snitterfield, but without much commitment: in 1561 he was fined for not looking after the hedges. John's future was not as a farmer but in trade. As well as leather, he bought and sold wool, barley and timber at various times. He also lent money to others, which may well have led to some of his future difficulties. In fact, his life shows both the opportunities and the dangers for the self-made men who created England's wealth in the sixteenth century.

This is the first known drawing of the Shakespeare house in Henley Street, Stratford, 1769.

A MAN OF PROPERTY

John Shakespeare became a man of property. When he bought the house next door in Henley Street in 1556, he converted them both into a single dwelling with large storerooms. That same year he bought a house with a garden and land in Greenhill Street in Stratford.

THE GOOD CITIZEN

In 1553, Stratford became a borough, legally able to manage its own affairs. As the town became more important, many new jobs were created. John became an official beer-taster in 1556. In 1558 he was a constable, helping to keep the peace, and in 1559 an affeeror, assessing the fines his fellow citizens had to pay. In 1561 he became a burgess, a 'town councillor', and then a chamberlain, in charge of the finances and property of the borough. In 1565 he was elected an alderman, a senior official, entitled to wear a fur-trimmed gown to church. Finally, in 1568, he was Bailiff, the 'mayor' of Stratford. There seemed no end to John Shakespeare's rise.

In 1575, John Shakespeare applied for a coat of arms, a sign of having 'made it' and something to which he was entitled as one-time Bailiff of Stratford. But changed circumstances meant he couldn't follow up the application until 1596. What went wrong? Nobody has ever been able to say exactly what it was, but we know that after 1575 – when his son, William, was eleven – John Shakespeare bought no more land, and stopped attending council business. By 1586, a new alderman was elected in his place because John Shakespeare 'dothe not come' to the council meetings 'nor hathe not done of Longe tyme'.

THINGS GO WRONG

Perhaps like many self-made men, John Shakespeare went too far, and the range of his dealings overstretched his finances. In 1569 he was accused of lending money to be repaid with interest – that is, he charged people to borrow money from him – which was then a criminal offence. Two years later he was accused of illegally buying large quantities of wool. But practices like these were part of the cut and thrust of successful business life at the time. Probably some of his deals went wrong. We know that John started selling land and property, presumably to raise money. But it is most likely that John Shakespeare was one of many victims of the sharp economic recession at the end of the sixteenth century.

In spite of the fact that John was heavily in debt in the 1590s and had to stay indoors for fear of arrest, he did not seem to lose the respect of his neighbours

Nevertheless, his decline must have been a blow, not least to his eldest child, William.

The last page of the Stratford Chamberlains' accounts, 1562–3. John Shakespeare's name appears near the bottom.

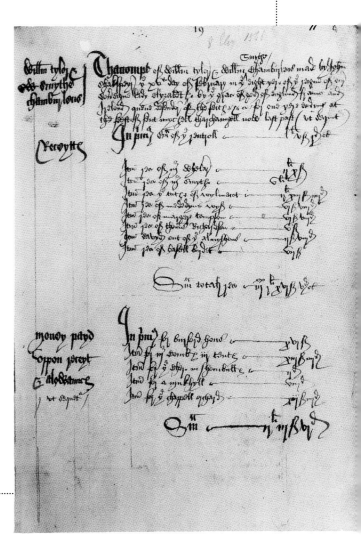

SHAKESPEARE AT SCHOOL

John Shakespeare's successful election as a Stratford burgess in 1561 allowed him to send any of his sons, free of charge, to the King's New School, King Edward VI's grammar school in the town. There is no certain proof, but William probably started at the grammar school when he was six (the usual age), after having learnt his alphabet and the Lord's Prayer, and perhaps simple arithmetic, at the petty ('little') school from the age of four. Some girls were probably also taught at the petty school (sewing rather than writing), but only boys went on to the grammar school.

THE LONG SCHOOL DAY

The school day in the sixteenth century was long and hard, beginning as early as six o'clock in the morning, with a two-hour lunch break from 11am until 1pm, and ending at 5pm: eight hours teaching a day. They had short breaks for breakfast and in the middle of the afternoon, and the day began and ended with prayers.

The schoolroom above the Guildhall in Stratford where Shakespeare was taught.

A woodcut showing schoolboys at work in an Elizabethan schoolroom.

Schoolwork at the grammar schools was based on the study of Latin, which was not only the language of Ancient Rome, but was also used by statesmen and scholars throughout Europe. Boys read and translated comedies by the Roman dramatists, Terence and Plautus, the political speeches of Cicero, the poems of Ovid, and dialogues by the modern author, Erasmus.

One big difference between then and now was that most of their work was spoken out loud. Indeed a teacher called Richard Mulcaster, who was headmaster of the Merchant Taylors' School in London, believed the best way to teach boys how to speak, argue and understand someone else's point of view was by acting out short scenes and dialogues. When Shakespeare was at the grammar school in Stratford, two of his masters were Thomas Jenkins (between 1575 and 1579) and John Cottom (1579 to about 1582). Jenkins had almost certainly been a pupil of Mulcaster and it is likely that he used his old master's teaching methods. If he did, we can see how, even as a boy, William would have begun to understand how to use words and arguments in lively and dramatic ways.

Jenkins was a Welshman. When Shakespeare wrote a comedy called *The Merry Wives of Windsor* (probably in 1597), he included a Welsh schoolmaster, Sir Hugh Evans, who in Act 4, scene 1, asks a boy to go through a Latin lesson. It is a hilarious scene, with the boy getting things wrong, and two lively and witty ladies deliberately finding rude alternative meanings for the Latin words. The boy's name is William. Is this a deliberate and fond memory of lessons back in Stratford between the Welsh teacher and a glover's son?

'**Evans:** *What is your genitive case plural, William?*

William: *Genitivo: "horum, harum, horum".*

Mistress Quickly: *Vengeance of Jenny's case! Fie on her! Never name her, child, if she be a whore.*'

PAGEANTS AND PROCESSIONS

In the days before film, television and radio, when there were no newspapers and less than half the population was able to read, information and entertainment had to be acted out. Kings, princes and nobles showed their wealth and power through processions and pageants – dramatic displays enacting a battle or historical scene, designed to impress their subjects.

THE ROYAL VISIT

In July 1575, Queen Elizabeth I visited Kenilworth Castle, the home of the Earl of Leicester, a few miles north of Stratford. She was nearly 42 years old, and unmarried. It's now thought that part of the Earl's plan was to persuade her to marry him, and he provided three magnificent weeks of entertainment to please and impress the Queen. There were fireworks and plays, hunting and bear-baiting – much of it taking place around the great lake at Kenilworth. The spectacle would have drawn people from miles around. Quite possibly Shakespeare, then an eleven-year-old glover's son, was among the crowds who saw a play about a battle between the English and the Danes performed by citizens of Coventry. He might also have seen a comic country wedding, and a pageant on the lake in which:

'Harry Goldingham was to represent Arion upon the Dolphin's back, but finding his voice to be very hoarse and unpleasant, he tears off his disguise and swears he was none of Arion, not he, but honest Harry Goldingham: which blunt discovery pleased the Queen better than if it had gone through in the right way.'

Perhaps it was at Kenilworth that Shakespeare first learned that truth about actors which Duke Theseus puts into words near the end of *A Midsummer Night's Dream:*

'The best in this kind are but shadows, and the worst are no worse if imagination amend them.'

The Church also used processions and plays to show how important it was and to present its teaching. Since 1311, a new religious festival had been kept – Corpus Christi – celebrated on a Thursday in June. The day quickly came to include a procession in which members of religious organizations and the various trade guilds (organizations for all tradesmen following a particular craft) took part. Eventually this procession developed into a cycle of plays called mystery plays showing the history of the world from Adam and Eve to the end of time.

A guild might perform a part of the Christian story that was particularly relevant to its own craft: the carpenters presenting the crucifixion of Jesus, for instance. One feature of these plays was the use of rough humour and realistic dialogue, bringing the Christian message into the everyday lives of performers and audience alike.

The very last performance of such a cycle of plays in England happened in Coventry – just a few miles from Stratford – in 1580, when Shakespeare was 16 years old. Was he there to watch? It's not impossible.

All great events were marked by spectacular processions. This is from a painting by D. van Asloot, 1615, in the Victoria and Albert Museum, London. It shows the entry of the Infanta Isabella into Brussels.

MARRIAGE AND FAMILY

When William Shakespeare was 18 years old, he married Anne Hathaway, a woman from Shottery (a mile west of Stratford), who was then aged about 26. There are two unusual things about this wedding. For a start, Shakespeare was a very young man. In the sixteenth century, the average age at which men usually married was between 24 and 28. Secondly, the marriage seems to have been arranged very quickly because a special licence was obtained from the Bishop of Worcester on 27 November 1582, allowing William and Anne to marry without the usual three weeks' public notice – given by an announcement in church, called 'publishing the banns'. There was a good reason for their speedy marriage: an entry in the Stratford parish registers tells us that 'Susanna daughter to William Shakespeare' was baptised on 26 May 1583. Anne must have already been three months' pregnant when they married.

From the time of their marriage until William bought New Place in Stratford in 1597, Anne and the children probably lived with William's parents in Henley Street. Susanna was followed by twins, a son Hamnet and a daughter Judith, baptised on 2 February 1585.

Holy Trinity Church, Stratford, where Shakespeare was baptised and buried.

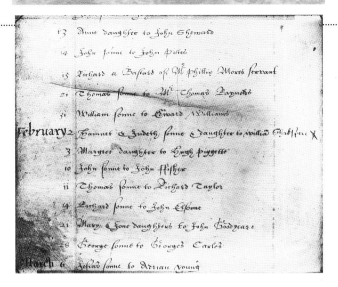

The record of the baptism of Judith and Hamnet Shakespeare on 2 February 1585.

A Busy Household

William Shakespeare's younger brothers and sisters would almost certainly have been living at Henley Street, too, when Anne moved in. Gilbert, born in October 1566, died a respectable and unmarried tradesman in February 1612. Joan, born in April 1569, outlived all her brothers and sisters, not dying until 1646. Anne, born in September 1571, had died in 1579. Almost nothing is known of Richard, except that he was born in March 1574 and died in February 1613. But Edmund, John and Mary Shakespeare's youngest child, born in May 1580, followed in his brother William's footsteps (see page 14), and went to London to become an actor. He died in 1607, and was buried on 31 December in the church of St Mary Overy (now Southwark Cathedral), very near to the Globe Theatre. The service took place in the morning, presumably so that his fellow actors could attend before their afternoon performance.

The Loss of his Son

When Hamnet Shakespeare was born, William would have been pleased that the Shakespeare family name would continue. But he died, aged eleven, and was buried in Stratford on 11 August 1596. We have nothing to tell us what his parents thought or felt when they lost their son. The bare records in the Stratford baptism and burial registers are all there is to mark out his life. The child's name, Hamnet, was not uncommon in Stratford at the time. But it must also remind us of another name – Hamlet, prince of Denmark and the doomed hero of one of Shakespeare's greatest plays, probably written in 1600, just four years after his son's death. In that play, a son sets out to avenge his father's murder. It is perhaps not too fanciful to suppose that when he was writing *Hamlet*, Shakespeare would have been painfully aware of the loss of his own son, Hamnet, whose death marked the end of the Shakespeare line.

THE UPSTART CROW

'THE LOST YEARS'

The time between William's marriage to Anne in 1582, and his appearance as a successful young playwright in London in 1592 are sometimes called 'the lost years'. What was he up to? How did he earn his living? Above all, how did the grammar school boy from Stratford get to London and start work with one of the more famous groups of actors?

One theory is that he became a tutor in the family of some great nobleman, perhaps in the north of England, perhaps on the introduction of his own teacher, John Cottom. From there he may have joined a company of actors – possibly the group called Lord Strange's Men – and travelled with them to London. It's possible, but we don't know.

THE QUEEN'S MEN

On the other hand, he could have met up with a company of actors in Stratford. We know that a number of companies played there when Shakespeare was a boy and a young man. One of these was the Queen's Men, who were paid twenty shillings (a good deal of money in those days) by the Stratford corporation to perform in 1587, when Shakespeare was 23. The Queen's Men had been formed in 1583 in a deliberate attempt to put the best actors in London under the direct control of Queen Elizabeth I and her Council. The company included the famous clowns, Richard Tarleton and Robert Wilson, as well as the 'straight' actors John Bentley and, until 13 June 1587, William Knell. On that day Knell was killed in a duel at Thame in Oxfordshire. We do not know whether the Queen's Men were on their way to Stratford, or had already been there, but one thing seems certain: they needed a new actor in a hurry. Was this when William Shakespeare got his first job?

A woodcut of 'the ghost of Robert Greene', who called Shakespeare an 'upstart crow'.

We can push this guesswork a bit further. It is very likely that Shakespeare's first play was the comedy, *Two Gentlemen of Verona*. In that play the character of Launce would have been played by the company's clown. Launce has a dog, Crab, and there is a very funny scene between the two of them. Now, we know that Richard Tarleton had a dog, and that he sometimes had 'conversations' with it as part of his act. Did Shakespeare write his first comic role for this master comedian and his dog? If he did, it would have been one of Tarleton's last roles because he died in 1588. And there are no more dogs in Shakespeare's plays.

The Queen's Men also performed the plays of Robert Greene, who provides us with another unusual piece of evidence that suggests Shakespeare was well known in London by 1592. In that year Greene wrote a sarcastic attack on a new, young writer: '. . . an upstart crow, beautified with our feathers, that with his Tiger's heart wrapped in a player's hide. . . is in his own conceit the only Shake-scene in a country.' This joke, using Shakespeare's name, is also being sarcastic about his ability to write plays.

Greene, educated at university, is attacking a grammar school boy for daring to compete as a playwright. Was this a severe case of sour grapes because Greene's work was no longer popular, or even because, some years earlier, Shakespeare's

The 'Ely Palace' portrait, said to be of William Shakespeare.

plays had started to replace his in the repertoire of the Queen's Men? Whatever the reason, by 1592 William Shakespeare was obviously successful enough to be attacked by other writers. Within two years he had enough money to buy himself a share in the Chamberlain's Men, the company of actors with whom he would work for the rest of his life.

THE PLAGUE, POEMS AND PATRONS

By the early 1590s Shakespeare had established himself as a playwright but his career was interrupted by that terrifyingly unpredictable fact of Elizabethan life – the bubonic plague. This terrible disease was spread by fleas carried by rats which thrived in the filthy living conditions of London and other cities.

The river Thames was an open sewer and people dumped their rubbish in the narrow streets. Anyone infected by the plague was isolated and left to die. The front doors of victims' houses were marked with a red cross. These marks, the cries of the dying and the creak of carts trundling through the streets carrying bodies towards the communal burial pits were dreadful sights and sounds of the time.

TOURING COMPANIES

There was a violent outbreak in 1592–3. Public meetings 'at plays, bear-baitings, bowlings and other like assemblies' were banned. Acting companies had to apply for licences to perform outside London. They may have carried the disease with them, and neither players nor audiences in country towns could have had much enthusiasm for the entertainment.

At this time, Shakespeare was probably a member of a touring company, but was also developing another kind of work. He was writing poems and arranging for them to be printed. The benefit of publishing his poetry was that he could earn money and attract the support of a wealthy patron who might open the door to other opportunities.

This woodcut of the plague in London shows how terrified people were of catching it.

FLATTERING HIS PATRON

In Shakespeare's time, any book that was printed was entered on a list known as the Stationers' Register. On 18 April 1593 Shakespeare's poem, *Venus and Adonis* was entered by its printer, Richard Field. He was a Stratford man who, like the poet, had made a successful move to London. *The Rape of Lucrece* was registered on 9 May 1594 by another printer, John Harrison. Both poems were dedicated to a young nobleman, Henry Wriothesley, Earl of Southampton, who was rich, dashing and influential. Shakespeare tried hard to win his patronage. Getting a patron meant gaining some financial support, protection, and an influential friend, all much needed in such unpredictable times. The dedications to the young earl follow the fashion of the time. They exaggerate his high position, making the poet very humble. Shakespeare wrote:

'. . . only if your honour seem but pleased, I account myself highly praised . . .'

He goes on to promise that if the earl likes the first poem, then something more serious will follow.

Venus and Adonis is an elegant and witty story based on a poem by Ovid, one of the Roman poets Shakespeare studied at school. He did not make a simple translation, but rewrote Ovid. He shows Venus, the goddess of love, chasing a bashful and inexperienced young man who finally escapes her advances to go hunting. It is both comic and sexy and was an immediate bestseller.

The Rape of Lucrece, also based on a story in Ovid, is more complex and serious. With these poems Shakespeare established his reputation as a versatile poet and began to attract the fashionable, aristocratic support he needed. This helped him financially and helped to make him successful.

A painting by John de Critz the Elder, 1603, of Henry Wriothesley, 3rd Earl of Southampton, who was Shakespeare's patron.

AT HOME IN LONDON

In October 1596, William Shakespeare was living in St Helen's parish in the City of London, the area today bounded by Bishopsgate Street, Houndsditch and Leadenhall Street, a little way north of the Tower of London. We know this because, in 1597, he was listed as among those from that parish who owed 5 shillings in unpaid tax. By 1600, when he still owed 13 shillings and 4 pence, the matter was referred to the Bishop of Winchester who was responsible for the 'Liberty of the Clink', that area on the south bank of the Thames where the Globe Theatre had been built in early 1599. This suggests that Shakespeare had now moved across the river to Southwark, to be nearer the new Theatre. He seems to have settled his tax debts because his name disappears from the lists by 1601.

SUCCESS

Shakespeare was a successful actor, poet, and playwright with a share in the profits of the Chamberlain's Men. Back in Stratford his father's situation was improving – with help from William's own money-making ventures perhaps? Within a year, the glover's son who'd left his home town to seek his fortune in London was able to buy the second largest house in Stratford – New Place – and install his wife and daughters there. Shakespeare had learned his trade – writing and acting – and was now in a position to profit from it.

A map of London at the end of the sixteenth century, showing the theatres.

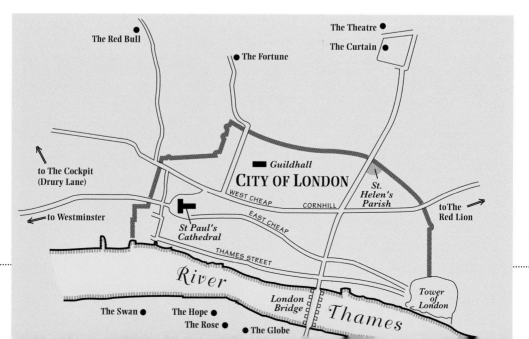

NEW PLAYHOUSES

In 1572 an 'Acte for the punishment of Vagabondes' (someone without a settled home) had made it necessary for companies of travelling actors to find the patronage of a powerful nobleman to protect them from possible arrest. A company led by James Burbage, a former carpenter, had been adopted by the Earl of Leicester. In 1576 Burbage leased part of the site of the old Holywell Priory, just north of the City of London, on the corner of what is now Curtain Road and New Inn Yard. There he built a permanent theatre for his company, and other companies visiting London. The Theatre, as it was called, was the second purpose-built playhouse in London. The first, the Red Lion, had been built in 1567 by Burbage's brother-in-law, John Brayne. Within a year of the completion of the Theatre another playhouse, the Curtain, was built almost next door, on the south side of what is now Holywell Lane. When Shakespeare was in London, he would have walked to one of these playhouses most days until the summer of 1599 when the Chamberlain's Men went across the river to the Globe.

A sketch of London Bridge, 1627, by Claude de Jongh. The Globe and Hope Theatres are on the far right.

THE EXCITEMENT OF THE CITY

London by Elizabethan standards was a huge city of over 200,000 people crammed into narrow streets and dark alleyways, criss-crossed by ditches and drains. A dangerous city of thieves, prostitutes, spies and confidence tricksters. A city of enormous contrasts, with the great wealth of nobility, royalty and rich merchants rubbing shoulders with utter poverty and degradation. A place of tremendous energy, where life could be lived to the full, not least because it could be snuffed out at any moment, by murder or disease.

The city was Shakespeare's second home. But unlike some of his fellow writers – Ben Jonson for example, or Thomas Dekker – Shakespeare didn't write much about London. His plays inhabit countries of the mind – imagined France or Italy, or more often what seems like rural Warwickshire recreated in a loving dream. If he did love London, he seems to have loved Stratford more.

THE CHAMBERLAIN'S MEN

SHAKESPEARE THE SHAREHOLDER

By the autumn of 1594 the worst of the plague was over, for a time at least, and normal life began again. The Lord Chamberlain asked the Lord Mayor of London to allow his company of actors to perform at the Cross Keys Inn in Gracechurch Street (near the present day monument to the Great Fire of London). In December, they played twice at the royal palace at Greenwich as part of the Queen's Christmas entertainment. The royal household accounts name three men who were paid for the company's performances: William Kemp, Richard Burbage and William Shakespeare, all described as 'servants to the Lord Chamberlain'. So, by the end of 1594, when Shakespeare was 30 years old, the company of actors with which he was now working was securely established as the Chamberlain's Men.

The group of men who worked together were experienced actors and, unlike previous companies, the Chamberlain's Men enjoyed many years of stability and success with few people joining or leaving. Shakespeare was one of those who bought a 'share' in the company.

He invested money (gained from the sale of his poems to the printers, perhaps, or with a gift from his patron, the Earl of Southampton) in return for a share in the profits. He worked hard to achieve the company's success as shareholder, actor and, of course, playwright.

The Chamberlain's Men performed plays by many writers but their special connection with Shakespeare was unusual for the time. He was the first 'resident playwright' in London, that is, he was employed to write especially for the company.

A portrait of Lord Chamberlain Hunsdon, 1591, which hangs in the National Portrait Gallery in London.

Frontispiece to Ben Jonson's play,
Every Man in His Humour,
in which Shakespeare acted.

SHAKESPEARE, COMPANY PLAYWRIGHT

Shakespeare wrote many different types of play for the company. He had made his mark as a writer of plays about English history, but he also developed the type of play known as a comedy. Shakespeare's comedies are not simply funny (though they often are very amusing). The word 'comedy' means that the play ends on a mainly hopeful note, reflecting a positive view of life. They are love stories, often complicated by misunderstandings which can be humorous or serious. The comedies of Shakespeare show the confusion and suffering which people can feel and cause in others as well as kindness, wit and high spirits. It is this wide range of human experience, and of types of character, which make them so attractive.

EVERY MAN IN his Humor.

As it hath beene sundry times publickly acted by the right Honorable the Lord Chamberlaine his seruants.

Written by BEN. IOHNSON.

Quod non dant proceres, dabit Histrio.

Haud tamen inuidias vati, quem pulpita pascunt.

Imprinted at London for *Walter Burre,* and are to be sould at his shoppe in Paules Church-yarde.
1601.

Shakespeare had the popular comic actor, Will Kemp, in the company, and made the most of his ability to entertain an audience. It is likely that Kemp first played Bottom in *A Midsummer Night's Dream.* Bottom is taken off by the Queen of the Fairies, treated like a king, given every luxury, then left alone. Was it only a dream? This part would have used Kemp's larger than life personality with great success.

It is hard for us to imagine ourselves as play-goers watching boy actors whose voices hadn't yet broken playing Shakespeare's female characters. The heroines of the comedies are usually very attractive, warm-hearted, quick-witted young women who run rings round the men. Twists in the stories often put them into situations where they disguise themselves as boys! Such confusion is the stuff of comedy.

THE GLOBE THEATRE

THE BURBAGE FAMILY

James Burbage and his sons, Richard and Cuthbert, played an important part in Shakespeare's life. As a boy, he would probably have seen James act with the Earl of Leicester's Men who brought plays to Stratford. James built the Theatre where many of Shakespeare's plays were first seen.

The Chamberlain's Men and its playwright were doing well there. Francis Meres, a young student, enjoyed going to plays and wrote admiringly in 1598:

'As Plautus and Seneca are accounted the best for comedy and tragedy among the Latins, so Shakespeare among the English is most excellent in both kinds for the stage.'

It would have been a blow to the company when they learnt that the lease on the land where the Theatre was built was not going to be renewed. Now the Theatre would have to be demolished. Where would they perform? The Burbages were not men to be put down easily. They painstakingly dismantled the Theatre, plank by plank, and used its timbers to build a magnificent large new playhouse on the south bank of the Thames.

The Globe opened in 1599. It was expensive to build and the Burbages could raise only fifty per cent of the cost themselves. Five of the shareholders in the company of the Chamberlain's Men, including Shakespeare, put up ten per cent each to make up the total sum. Shakespeare had evidently earned well in the 1590s and as a shareholder in the Globe he was in line to receive greater profits than before. He was not only a successful man in the theatre but in business, too.

There was a productive relationship between Shakespeare and Richard Burbage, the leading actor who first played many of the most demanding roles including the leads in the plays *Hamlet*, *Othello* and *King Lear*. These plays are called tragedies and explore suffering and the clash between good and evil, hope and despair, love and conflict. They make huge demands on the actor's emotions and understanding. Shakespeare must have been very confident of Burbage's ability. It's likely, too, that the actor's comments and questions affected the script which was eventually performed, just as playwrights today often adjust their plays during rehearsal. Shakespeare and Burbage worked together as business partners and artists for at least twenty years.

But it wasn't all tragedy on the stage of the Globe. The comedies and the plays based on English history or accounts of the leaders of Ancient Greece and Rome were also popular. In his plays Shakespeare raised questions about the qualities needed in a good king, and the rights and wrongs of opposition to a bad or weak one. Such questions might have been explored on stage using all the glamour of the past, but they were real and urgent in Elizabethan London, where the Queen was old and had no heir.

They were no less relevant when the new king, James I, came to the throne in 1603 and the Chamberlain's Men, renamed the King's Men, had a special role to play in performing before the Court, where their plays would have been the subject of intense debate.

In the outdoor theatres, audiences were large, noisy, enthusiastic, but no less responsive and critical. Even foreign visitors found the theatre one of the most exciting elements of city life, as they still do today!

The Globe theatre: a drawing based on Cornelius de Visscher's view of London, 1616.

DANGEROUS TIMES

Acting companies lived on the fringes of court life. As intelligent, literate men of the world they were easily caught up in the political and diplomatic intrigues that marked the later years of the reign of Queen Elizabeth and the first years of King James. They also had freedom of movement, not only throughout England when they went on tour, but on the mainland of Europe as well. Above all, plays were an important source of information and propaganda – a way of influencing opinion. There was always the danger that performances might cause a disturbance.

Actors and playwrights might be available to act as spies or secret messengers, but even though they could be used by the politicians, they still had to be kept under control.

A very good example of the way actors and writers got involved in politics can be seen in the career of Christopher Marlowe, a university man, a poet, and the writer of startlingly original plays in the 1580s and 1590s: *Doctor Faustus*, *Tamburlaine the Great* and *The Jew of Malta*. Marlowe died mysteriously in a fight in a tavern at Deptford on Wednesday 30 May 1593. The story was put around that it was simply the result of an argument about the bill, but recent research has brought to light many more facts. It now seems that Marlowe was almost certainly involved in some spying activity and that he was killed because he was getting in the way of the political ambitions of the Earl of Essex.

Sir Francis Walsingham, Queen Elizabeth's spymaster. This portrait in the National Portrait Gallery is said to be by John de Critz the Elder, c 1585.

The Chamberlain's Men were involved with the Earl of Essex a few years later. By 1601, the Earl was becoming desperate in his attempts to be the Queen's favourite, and even her husband. He made his move on 7 February 1601, threatening a rebellion. His failure was total and he was executed three weeks later. The day before the rebellion started, the plotters had gone to the Globe Theatre where they attended a specially arranged performance of Shakespeare's *Richard II*, a play about rebellion and the killing of a king. The Chamberlain's Men managed to avoid any punishment for their innocent involvement in Essex's activities, and in fact performed at Court again on 24 February, the night before the Earl's execution. But there must have been anxious moments as the investigation went on.

THE STATE CENSOR

Whenever a company wished to put on a new play, they had to send its text to an official of the court, the Lord Chamberlain who, with his assistant, the Master of the Revels, was responsible for all public performances. They often rejected plays, or demanded cuts in the text or the rewriting of scenes. In 1605, a play called *Eastward Ho!*, written by Ben Jonson, George Chapman and John Marston was performed, but a few lines which seemed to be insulting the Scots gave offence to King James who was himself Scottish.

The authors were imprisoned and only released when influential friends spoke up for them.

Some years earlier, probably in 1592 or 1593, a group of writers had begun a play about a famous Englishman in the days of Henry VIII, Sir Thomas More. When the play landed on the desk of Sir Edward Tilney, Master of the Revels, he was unhappy that one of its themes was an attack on foreigners living in London, just at a time when this had once more become a source of tension. He demanded rewrites and it looks as though Shakespeare was called in – perhaps as much as ten years later – to help, but Tilney still had objections and the play was never performed.

Ben Jonson – actor and playwright. He once killed a man, and was later put in prison for his part in writing a play which offended King James I.

A SUCCESSFUL BUSINESSMAN

It is very easy to see William Shakespeare as simply a great playwright and a genius in his use of the English language. He was both of these but all the time he remained a clever and hard-headed businessman, committed to making money for himself and his family. His father was a master glover, a merchant, a property owner, a dealer in a variety of raw materials, and a significant figure in the running of his home town of Stratford-upon-Avon. William Shakespeare was a man of trade, too – his craft was words, his skill lay in the new world of the London theatre. But like his father, he seems to have used his wealth in a variety of ways. One of the things that made William determined to be successful was quite possibly a wish to restore the good name of the Shakespeare family in Stratford since his father's decline in fortune.

NEW PLACE

William Shakespeare bought New Place in Stratford on 4 May 1597 for £60 in silver. This, 'the second biggest house in Stratford', was built at the end of the fifteenth century by Sir Hugh Clopton, another Stratford man who had prospered in London, becoming Lord Mayor in 1492. Shakespeare's wife and family moved in and by the time the playwright himself began to spend most of his time in Stratford – around 1610 – they had acquired other property in the town, including 107 acres of land at Welcombe on its northern boundary. There has often been speculation that William and Anne had an unhappy marriage, but to judge from the way his affairs prospered throughout these years, she must have been a good business partner, much like her mother-in-law, Mary. Shakespeare's eldest daughter, Susanna, was married in 1607 to a doctor, John Hall. They lived at New Place with her parents after the marriage and had a daughter, Elizabeth, who was born in 1608, and lived until 1670. Elizabeth was the last direct relative of William Shakespeare.

An early drawing of New Place, Stratford, which Shakespeare bought in 1597.

William Shakespeare.
Died April 23rd 1616. 52 Years Old.

William Shakespeare,
the 'Flower Portrait'.

THE GLOBE BURNS DOWN

In March 1613, Shakespeare even bought some property in London – part of the gatehouse of the Blackfriars – on the north bank of the Thames, not far from his company's indoor theatre. But disaster struck on 29 June of that year. During a performance of the play *Henry VIII*, probably written by Shakespeare with the younger writer John Fletcher, the thatched roof was set alight and the Globe Theatre burnt down. Within a year it was rebuilt but with a new resident playwright – John Fletcher. William Shakespeare seems to have written nothing more for his theatre.

Throughout his time in London, William Shakespeare continued his links with Stratford. In 1598 a neighbour from home, Richard Quiney, seems to have persuaded William to lend him and his partner Abraham Sturley some money to help them with a business venture. Similarly, once he had moved back to Stratford there were still links with London: the King's Men needed his business sense as well as his playwriting skills.

WILL AND DEATH

On 6 July, 1614 a great fire swept through the narrow streets and timber-framed houses of Stratford. It was a devastating blow to many families, causing much loss of property, livelihood and prosperity. Although New Place was not damaged, the Shakespeares must have felt the effects on the economy of the town.

ENCLOSURE

In an attempt to recoup their losses, some Stratford landowners decided to follow a national trend and make changes to the way they farmed their land. The detail of this change – called 'enclosure' – is complicated, but basically it meant that large landowners evicted tenants from their property and turned the land over to cheaper types of farming. The result was widespread poverty and unemployment among the small tenant farmers, but increased profits for the owners of the land.

In Stratford, there was a group led by Thomas Combe, Arthur Mainwaring and William Replingham in favour of enclosure, while another, led by a lawyer, Thomas Greene, opposed them. It's not clear whose side Shakespeare was on.

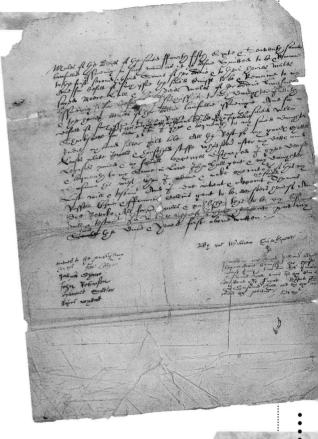

The final page of Shakespeare's will, 1616, showing his signature.

As a landowner he would have had a lot to gain; but he also seems to have come to the conclusion that the supporters of enclosure would never get their scheme off the ground. He was right. In spite of bullying tactics by Thomas Combe and some tricky negotiating by Replingham, the enclosure proposals were defeated in a court of law. But that was not until 1619, and by then Shakespeare had been dead for three years.

PROVIDING FOR HIS FAMILY

In the middle of this bitter disagreement – which caused much anger and distress in Stratford – Shakespeare drew up his will. This was in January 1616. The next month his daughter, Judith, was married – she was 31. Judith married Thomas Quiney, a Stratford wine merchant. In January, William's will included a bequest of £100 to Thomas. But he proved to be a doubtful character. Judith was already pregnant when they married and in March another woman claimed to be having his baby as well. She and the child died in childbirth that month and Thomas Quiney was punished by the Church for his offence. William Shakespeare rewrote his will to exclude Quiney – only Judith inherited the £100, and a few other things including 'a broad silver and gilt bowl'.

Even though she was provided for, Judith's share was much less than that of her elder sister, Susanna, and her husband, Dr John Hall. They inherited New Place, the other properties and most of the contents of the houses, presumably including Shakespeare's books. Shakespeare's sister, Joan, got £20 and his clothes, her sons were left £5 each.

Other friends and relatives received small gifts, but the best-known bequest was that to his wife: she was to have 'the second-best bed'.

People have often taken this as a sign that William and Anne did not get on, but we have no reason to think that. Since a widow usually remained in her own home after the death of her husband, no special arrangement was needed. And since the best bed was reserved for guests, the 'second-best bed' was the one she had slept in all her married life.

These arrangements were made just in time. On 23 April 1616 William Shakespeare died at home in Stratford. He was exactly 52 years old.

The monument to Shakespeare in Holy Trinity Church, Stratford.

FAME AND THE FIRST FOLIO

Shakespeare also left small sums of money to his actor friends Richard Burbage, John Hemmings and Henry Condell, with which they were to buy rings to remember the man who had helped them achieve fame and fortune on the stage. They repaid his friendly gesture by an act which was to guarantee that Shakespeare's reputation lived on long after he himself had died: they arranged to have a collected edition of his plays printed.

THE FIRST COLLECTION OF PLAYS

The First Folio, published in 1623, contains 36 of the 37 plays generally agreed to have been written by Shakespeare. Eighteen of these had not been printed before, while the others had appeared earlier as individual texts known as Quartos. (Folio and Quarto refer to the size of the paper used by the printers.) A copy of a new First Folio would have cost you £1 in 1623 (which was equivalent to a month's wages for a skilled worker), and it came without a cover so you would have paid out more for a leather binding. If one of the 250 copies surviving today were to change hands, it would sell for about a million pounds.

Burbage died in 1619 leaving Hemmings and Condell to sort out the scripts. They had several possible sources: prompt book copies of the whole plays which would have been used at the Globe or the Blackfriars Theatres – these may even have been Shakespeare's own original copies; the actors' individual parts written out on long scrolls of paper; and earlier printed versions. Some of the plays had been performed regularly for many years, others were virtually forgotten; in bringing them all together in one large book Hemmings and Condell were celebrating a brilliant man of the theatre. They were also making sure that the King's Men would continue to profit from his genius.

William Shakespeare was buried in the parish church in Stratford. There is still a monument to him there with its famous inscription:

'Reader, for Jesus' Sake forbear

To dig the dust enclosed here:

*Blessed be he
that spares these Stones,*

*And cursed be he
that moves my bones.'*

His statue looks out at us, holding a quill pen. It is the symbol of his art and craft, but also of his trade – the way he made his money, restored his father's good name and supported his wife and family.

At the beginning of the First Folio, poems and letters from a number of Shakespeare's admirers tried to say something about his genius. One of his fellow playwrights, Ben Jonson, who had himself published his *Collected Works* in 1616, understood better than most that Shakespeare's life and work could never be separated from the need to survive and prosper in the often dangerous and always insecure world of the theatre. But it was Jonson who recognised that Shakespeare was more than just a man of his time. In his poem in the First Folio Jonson wrote:

> *'Thou art a Monument,*
> *without a tomb,*
>
> *And art alive still,*
> *while thy Booke doth live,*
>
> *And we have wits to read,*
> *and praise to give . . .'*

William Shakespeare, on the Frontispiece of the First Folio.

INDEX